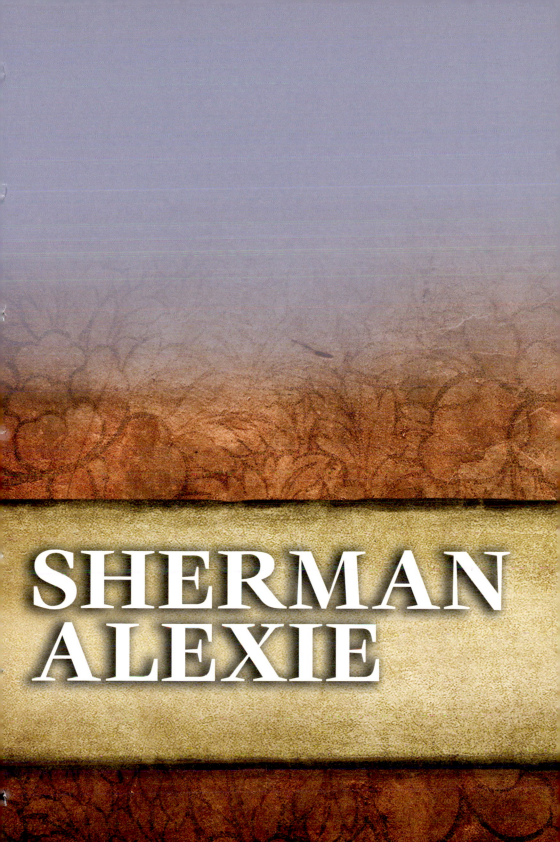

SHERMAN ALEXIE

ALL ABOUT THE AUTHOR™

SHERMAN
ALEXIE

LIZ SONNEBORN

ROSEN
PUBLISHING®

New York

Published in 2013 by The Rosen Publishing Group, Inc.
29 East 21st Street, New York, NY 10010

Library of Congress Cataloging-in-Publication Data

Sonneborn, Liz.
Sherman Alexie/Liz Sonneborn.—1st ed.
    p. cm.—(All about the author)
Includes bibliographical references and index.
ISBN 978-1-4488-6941-1 (library binding)
1. Alexie, Sherman, 1966—Juvenile literature. 2. Indians of
North America—Biography—Juvenile literature. 3. Authors,
American—20th century—Biography—Juvenile literature.
I. Title.
PS3551.L35774Z86 2012
818'.5409—dc23
                                                    2011039479

Manufactured in the United States of America

CPSIA Compliance Information: Batch #S12YA: For further information, contact Rosen Publishing, New York,
New York, at 1-800-237-9932.

CONTENTS

INTRODUCTION 6

CHAPTER ONE   GROWING UP 9

CHAPTER TWO   BECOMING A WRITER 26

CHAPTER THREE   FINDING SUCCESS 39

CHAPTER FOUR   WRITING FOR YOUNG READERS 54

CHAPTER FIVE   TELLING STORIES 66

FACT SHEET ON SHERMAN ALEXIE 81

FACT SHEET ON SHERMAN
ALEXIE'S WORK 83

CRITICAL REVIEWS 88

TIMELINE 91

GLOSSARY 93

FOR MORE INFORMATION 96

FOR FURTHER READING 100

BIBLIOGRAPHY 103

INDEX 107

Fourteen-year-old Sherman Alexie was sitting in a classroom in his school on the Spokane Indian Reservation. He opened a beaten-up math textbook and saw something that made him furious. It was his mother's maiden name—the name she used before she had married his father.

Sherman knew exactly what it meant. This was the very same book that his mother had used for her math lessons when she was a girl. How can I learn anything here, Sherman wondered, if my textbook is thirty years old? Mad at the school and mad at his life, Sherman grabbed the book and threw it. It sailed through the air before slamming against a wall with a dull thud.

Twenty-seven years later, Sherman Alexie was sitting in another room, in New York City, far from the Indian reservation in Washington State where he grew up. In this hotel ballroom, he was surrounded by many of the greatest American writers of the day. They were all there waiting for the announcement of the winners of the 2007 National Book Award.

Alexie was one of the nominees for the award for young people's literature. His acclaimed novel *The Absolutely True Diary of a Part-Time Indian* was inspired by the problems, struggles, and occasional triumphs he experienced as a teenager. The book's hero, Arnold Spirit Jr., threw a math book just as

In 2007, Sherman Alexie won the National Book Award for his first novel for young readers, *The Absolutely True Diary of a Part-Time Indian*. The National Book Award is one of the most prestigious prizes an American writer can win.

young Alexie had done. But in Arnold's case the book hit a teacher, an event that set Arnold off on an adventure that took him away from the reservation and into the wider world.

Novelist Elizabeth Partridge read the names of the nominees of the young people's literature award. She then paused and announced the winner—Sherman Alexie. He moved through the audience and bounded onto the stage, smiling as he told the audience, "Wow! Well, I obviously should have been writing YA [young adult literature] all along!" During his acceptance speech, available for viewing on the National Book Foundation's Web site, he remembered how as a college student reading a poem by Adrian C. Louis, a Paiute Indian poet, had changed his life. It suggested to him that he—a poor kid from the Spokane Indian Reservation—might be able to be a writer, too. "It's been a gorgeous and lonely and magical and terrifying twenty years since then," he told the audience.

Because of the success of *True Diary*, many readers think of Alexie as just a YA author. Although he enjoys this new role, he had a long career before putting Arnold Spirit's story into print. Alexie has been a poet, a short story writer, a novelist, a screenwriter, a comedian, and a musician. But no matter what medium he works in, Alexie attracts fans who love exploring the gorgeous, lonely, magical, and terrifying worlds he creates.

GROWING UP

When Sherman Joseph Alexie Jr. was born on October 7, 1966, hardly any-one thought he would live to see his first birthday. He was diagnosed with hydro-cephalus, a condition in which too much fluid causes the brain to swell. The boy's doctors decided to operate when he was only six months old. They told Alexie's parents that the brain surgery would likely have one of two outcomes. In the worst case, their baby would die. In the best, he would be severely mentally impaired for the rest of his life.

Despite the doctors' dire predictions, Alexie not only survived, but he also came through the surgery with his ability to think and reason fully intact. The incident

ONE

NORMAL ANATOMY

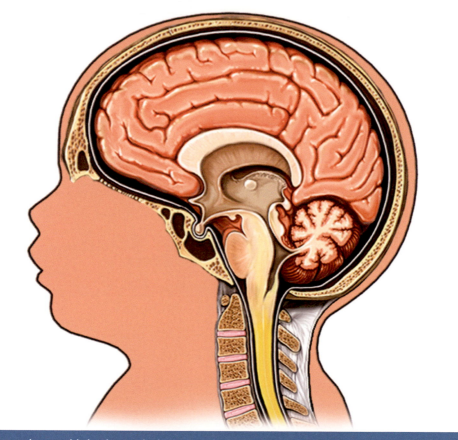

Alexie was born with hydrocephalus, popularly known as "water on the brain." This life-threatening condition, caused by too much fluid in a person's head, causes the brain to swell and push out against the skull.

established a pattern that would repeat itself throughout Alexie's life. Through luck and determination, he would again and again defy others' low expectations of what he could do.

HYDROCEPHALIC CONDITION

OUTWARD PRESSURE
OF BRAIN EXPANDS
SKULL CAVITY

CONTINUED
PRESSURE PUSHES
BRAIN OUT THROUGH
BOTTOM OF SKULL
(ARNOLD-CHIARI
MALFORMATION)

ON THE RESERVATION

Even though the operation was a success, Alexie
was ill throughout much of his childhood. He had
seizures until he was seven years old. The seizures

were terrifying, but they could also leave him feeling exhilarated. In a 2008 interview published in the British newspaper the *Guardian*, he explained that, during a seizure, "there's a surreal euphoria; the synapses are misfiring, so the memory banks are flooding your head. I'd get to feel like a superhero for a couple of minutes." On heavy medication, Alexie spent much of his youth in and out of hospitals.

Poor health was far from the only obstacle Alexie faced. Growing up on Washington's Spokane Indian Reservation was often difficult. His father, Sherman, was a member of the Coeur d'Alene tribe. His mother, Lillian, was of mixed ancestry. She had ancestors from three Indian groups— the Spokane, Colville, and Flathead. Through one grandfather, she was also one-quarter white. The couple had six children, including Alexie. Raising such a large family would be a challenge under any conditions, but it was especially hard on the reservation. Like nearly all its residents, the Alexie family was desperately poor.

Alexis grew up in the town of Wellpinit on the Spokane Indian Reservation, which is located along the Spokane River in eastern Washington State. The city of Spokane lies to the east of the reservation.

Living in Wellpinit, the reservation's only town, money was hard to come by. Alexie's mother worked in Wellpinit's one store while earning a little on the side by selling handmade quilts. His father was a laborer who often found odd jobs driving trucks or working in the logging industry.

Both his parents also severely abused alcohol. As Alexie explained in 2007 on the radio show *Morning Edition*, "On my reservation, in my family, alcoholism was epidemic." Nearly all of his many relatives on the reservation had drinking problems. Some even died of alcohol-related illnesses or accidents. The death that most affected Alexie was that of his eldest sister. When he was a teenager, her trailer home caught fire and, in an alcoholic haze, she was unable to escape. Alexie later recalled that, after hearing the news of her death, he could not stop crying for weeks.

FATHER AND SON

Alexie's mother eventually came to terms with her drinking problem and even became a counselor for other recovering alcoholics on the reservation. His father, however, continued to drink until he died of alcohol-related kidney failure in 2004. His alcohol abuse cast a pall over Alexie's entire childhood. For long stretches, his father would not drink at all, although Alexie told the *Guardian* in 2008 that even

AMERICAN INDIANS AND ALCOHOLISM

One of the most hateful stereotypes applied to American Indians is that all Indians are alcoholics. In fact, the vast majority of Indians do not abuse alcohol. Many do not drink at all. But for some Indians, particularly those living on reservations, alcoholism—their own or that of their friends or relatives—is an enormously destructive force in their lives. According to the National Institute on Alcohol Abuse and Alcoholism's publication "American Indians and Alcohol," Indians are four times more likely than the general population to contract cirrhosis, a serious liver disease linked to excessive alcohol use. American Indians are also three times more likely to die in alcohol-related car accidents; 1.4 times, in alcohol-related suicides; and 2.5 times, in alcohol-related homicides.

then his father "was always depressed. When he was home and sober, he was mostly in his room." His father was an insomniac, which gave rise to some of Alexie's most tender memories of him. In 2002, on the television show *Now with Bill Moyers*, he explained: "My father was sleepless most of his life. So by the age of five, I was awake with him all night long, watching bad television or we'd lie in the same bed, and I'd read my comic books while he read his latest spy or mystery novel."

THE SPOKANE INDIANS

For centuries, the Spokane Indians lived along a large stretch of the Spokane River in what is now eastern Washington State and northern Idaho. They obtained most of their food by fishing in the waters of the Spokane and Columbia rivers.

The Spokane first encountered non-Indians in the early 1800s. For years, they traded peacefully with these newcomers. But, over time, settlers and miners began taking control over their homeland. Outbreaks of smallpox, a disease introduced by non-Indians, also greatly reduced the Spokane's population.

In the late nineteenth century, the U.S. government confined the Spokane to several small Indian reservations, including the Spokane Indian Reservation in Washington. The Spokane tribe now has approximately 2,500 members, with about half making their home on this reservation.

In addition to Sherman Alexie, noted members of the Spokane tribe include Gloria Bird and Charlene Teters. Gloria Bird is a poet who helped found the Northwest Native American Association. She is also the co-editor of the anthology *Reinventing the Enemy's Language: Contemporary Native Women's Writing of North America* (1998). Charlene Teters is a professor at the Institute of American Indian Arts in Santa Fe, New Mexico. She is best known for speaking out against the use of American Indian mascots by sports teams.

A Spokane man wears traditional ceremonial clothing during a powwow held on the Spokane Indian Reservation. Powwows are festivals, often held on reservations, at which people gather to enjoy American Indian music, food, and dancing.

His father's recreational reading helped introduce Alexie to the world of books. As he told the *Guardian* in 2008, "My dad…loved books: genre stuff—westerns, mysteries, true crime, conspiracy theory. I loved my dad, so his obsessions became mine."Alexie's father was particularly obsessed with books that questioned

The people of the Spokane Indian tribe traditionally lived along the Spokane River in present-day eastern Washington and northern Idaho. They obtained much of their food by fishing the waters of the Spokane and Columbia rivers.

the official account of the assassination of President John F. Kennedy in 1963. Sharing his father's enthusiasms, Alexie as a boy built a model of Dealey Plaza, where the assassination took place, out of Lego blocks.

When he was home, Alexie's father was often a loving parent. But he frequently disappeared for

days or even weeks on drinking binges. His behavior left Alexie unsettled, causing him to worry and wonder when his father might reappear. "I'd lie awake at night waiting for him to come home," he explained on *Now with Bill Moyers*. The anxiousness he felt in childhood stayed with him even after he grew up: "[M]aybe I learned how to be an insomniac because I'm still waiting for my father to come home."

A LOVE OF READING

Plagued by illness and family troubles, Alexie found comfort in books. By age three, he could read. By the time he was in kindergarten, he was poring over adult literature, including such weighty material as *The Grapes of Wrath*, John Steinbeck's classic novel of the Great Depression. In a 2009 interview on SouthCoastToday.com, Alexie recalled: "I read all of Steinbeck. Most of [Ernest] Hemingway. [George Orwell's] *Animal Farm*, but also [the children's book] *Harold and the Purple Crayon*, and stuff for kids my age. I just read everything; I wanted pages. Pages, stories. Anything." By the time he was twelve, Alexie had read every book in the reservation library.

Reading not only helped him pass the time. It also provided a mental escape from reservation life, which felt more stifling the older Alexie got. Most reservation residents had lived there all their lives.

As Alexie explained in the SouthCoastToday.com interview: "I grew up in a monoculture. I grew up in a house half a mile [0.8 kilometer] from the house where my mom was born. My mom was born in the house where her mother was born. When we have family reunions on the rez [slang for "reservation"], you just have to walk out the door and throw a rock, and you'll hit a cousin." Few people he knew ever left the reservation or even thought much about the world beyond it. The widespread poverty and alcohol abuse on the reservation wore Alexie down. But he came to find the lack of curiosity about other places and other people the most difficult thing about living there. As Alexie put it, he could not cope with the "[l]ack of hope. All around me. The lack of a need to move. Lack of wanderlust."

FRUSTRATED IN SCHOOL

His school provided little relief. Alexie was routinely teased by the other kids, who nicknamed him "the Globe" because of his enlarged skull that resulted from hydrocephalus. He was also mocked for the large horn-rimmed glasses he had been issued by the Indian Health Service, the federal agency that provides health care to Indian groups.

Even worse was the school building itself, which to Alexie was a symbol of the grim sense of hopelessness that overwhelmed his classmates. As

Sherman Alexie began his college career at Gonzaga University, a Catholic university in Spokane, Washington. He received a scholarship to Gonzaga because of his strong high school record. In high school, Alexie was an honor student and the captain of the basketball team.

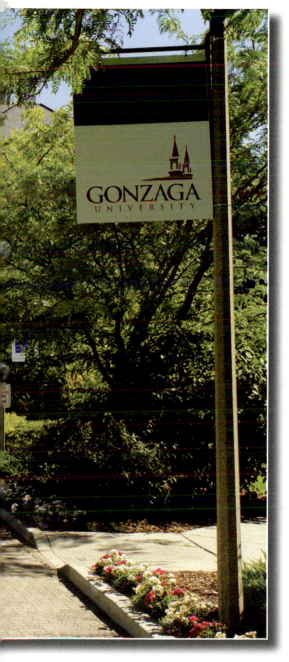

he explained in his essay "Every Teen's Struggle," which appeared in *Publishers Weekly* in 2008, "My reservation school was an inglorious, ancient, gigantic and decrepit brick building stuffed with asbestos, mice, mold and Spokane Indian kids who would never take the SAT."

He decided to do something no one he knew had ever done—transfer to a high school off the reservation. The nearest one was Reardan High School, located in a farming town more than 20 miles (32 km) away from his home. The idea of transferring seemed crazy to his family members, none of whom had spent much time off the reservation. Alexie told SouthCoastToday.com that, looking back, he was still amazed at how bold he had been as a teen: "You can only do [something like] that when you're 14. I'm marveled by that kid. Everything he did."

TAKING CHARGE

The physical distance between his home and new school was daunting because he did not have regular access to a car. He had to bum rides or sometimes even walk the whole way. But the psychological distance between the two places was even greater. On the reservation, nearly everyone was an Indian living in poverty. At Reardan, most of the students were middle-class whites. For Alexie, it was like traveling between two completely different worlds.

When he enrolled, Alexie had no idea what to expect from his new classmates. But, to his surprise, even though he was the only Indian in the school, he experienced fairly little discrimination. Instead, he quickly found friends based on shared interests, particularly books and basketball. In time, he became the star player on the high school basketball team, ironically called the Reardan Indians. Alexie also excelled in his classes. By the time he graduated, he was an honor student and basketball team captain. His high school record was so good that he earned a full-scholarship to Gonzaga University in Spokane, Washington.

In just a few years, Alexie had gone from reservation kid to college student. Even as an adult, he was impressed by his journey. In his *Publishers Weekly* essay, he explained, "It might sound self-mythologizing, but my flight across the reservation border was an outrageous and heroic act. Even now, I can't believe I had the courage to do it."

TWO

CHAPTER

BECOMING A WRITER

Sherman Alexie began his studies at Gonzaga, a Catholic university in Spokane, in 1985. After spending so much of his youth around doctors and hospitals, he decided to pursue a career in medicine. But Alexie quickly learned he probably was not cut out to be a doctor. Early on, he fainted three times during a human anatomy class.

Alexie also had trouble fitting in at the school, where many of the students were white people from wealthy backgrounds. He took to making fun of his hard-partying classmates and their drunken behavior, giving them mocking Indian-style names like Vomiting Eagle and Asleep-in-the-Bathroom. Alexie was proud that he never drank in high school, but his social discomfort and the pressure to succeed at

Gonzaga chipped away at his resolve to stay away from alcohol. As he told *Writer* magazine, "I guess I was just a lot more confident as a 16-year-old than I was as a 19-year-old. I was scared [in college]. Alcohol numbs fears." Drinking as much as a case of beer a day, Alexie dropped out of school in 1987.

DISCOVERING INDIAN LITERATURE

Miserable and adrift, Alexie moved to Seattle, Washington, where he got a job busing tables at a sandwich shop. He eventually decided to give college another try. Alexie enrolled at Washington State University in Pullman.

On a whim, Alexie signed up for a creative writing class. He figured that the class might teach him how to write poetry that would impress girls. But the class gave him much more—a calling in life and a brand new career path.

Alexie's instructor was Alex Kuo, a professor and poet of American Indian descent. After his first assignment, Kuo recognized that Alexie had the potential to become an accomplished writer. To encourage Alexie, Kuo gave him a copy of *Songs from This Earth on Turtle's Back* (1983). The book was an anthology of poems and other works by contemporary American Indian poets, including

A member of the Blackfeet and Gros Ventre tribes, James Welch (1940–2003) was a poet and novelist best known for his award-winning book *Fools Crow* (1986). He was an inspiring figure for the next generation of American Indian writers, which included Sherman Alexie.

Leslie Silko, James Welch, Adrian C. Louis, and Joy Harjo. It was edited by Joseph Bruchac, an Abenaki Indian whose work as a writer and editor has been instrumental in introducing the reading public to American Indian literature.

The collection was a revelation to Alexie. "It was the first time I'd seen anything creative by an Indian," he explained to the *Guardian* in 2008. It not only introduced him to the notion that American Indians could be creative artists. It also showed him that the life he had known as a boy was a legitimate subject for literature. In a 2005 interview published in the scholarly journal *MELUS*, he explained, "Before I read that book I had no idea that you could write about Indian life with powwows, ceremonies, broken down cars, cheap motels; all this stuff that was my life as I was growing up on the reservation."

EMBRACING POETRY

Alexie was also drawn to the medium of poetry. He began spending time in the college library, poring over poetry journals, trying to learn everything he could about modern poets and their work. He felt an immediate connection to them, as he told *MELUS*: "Before, I had always thought that I was a freak in the way I saw and felt about the world. As I started reading the works of all these poets I realized that I, at least, wasn't the only freak!"

Armed with his new knowledge, Alexie began to write his own poems at a furious pace. Kuo told him he should try submitting them to poetry magazines for publication. One of the poetry magazines Alexie approached was *Hanging Loose*, which is published in Brooklyn, New York. An editor there named Bob Hershon read his submissions. According to a 2003 article published in the *Guardian*, Hershon said he immediately recognized that Alexie was a "promising young writer," adding that "we soon started thinking— this kid is really good."

In 1990, a few of Alexie's poems were published in *Hanging Loose*. The editors then decided to publish a book-length collection of Alexie's work. Learning that his first book was to be published was a life-changing moment for Alexie. The news made him decide to quit drinking, and he has been sober ever since. In his 2008 *Guardian* interview, Alexie maintained the decision was motivated by "arrogance": "I had the feeling I was going to be successful, and I didn't want to be another disappointing Indian. The mess my father was, it broke my heart. I didn't want to break an Indian kid's heart."

FINDING AN AUDIENCE

Alexie received his bachelor's degree in American studies from Washington State University in 1994, although he stopped taking classes in 1991. In 1992, two collections of his poems—*The Business of Fancydancing* and *I Would Steal Horses*—were published. Books of poetry usually have a tiny audience. But through word of mouth, Alexie's work, particularly *Fancydancing*, was finding readers, especially in the Pacific Northwest.

Poetry lovers were not the only people taking notice of Alexie. He was also attracting attention from some of the most influential critics in the country. Based on *Fancydancing*, many declared that Alexie was an important new writer on the literary scene.

The acclaim was dizzying for Alexie. He was stunned and a little frightened about the praise heaped on him and his work. Alexie was especially

Alexie has built a large audience for his work through public readings, such as this one in Portland, Oregon, which was broadcast on the *Live Wire!* radio show in 2009.

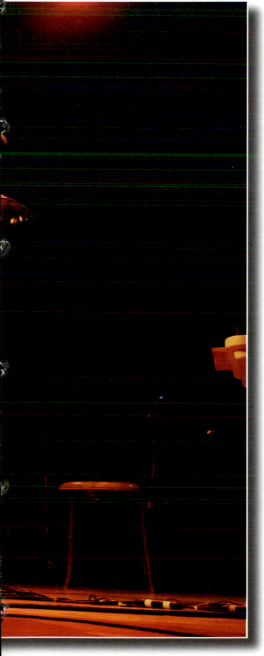

startled by a 1992 *New York Times Book Review* article that took a look at the state of modern American Indian literature. It declared that Alexie was "one of the major lyric voices of our time." When he read the article, he was so overwhelmed that he rushed into a bathroom and threw up.

Not everyone reviewed his early work so positively. Some critics, particularly American Indian writers, complained that his many references to alcohol and alcoholism were promoting the stereotype that all Indians are alcoholics. Alexie argued that he was merely writing about what he knew. As he told *MELUS* in 2005, "People thought I was writing about stereotypes, but more than anything I was writing about my own life."

PERFORMING LITERATURE

As soon as his first book was published, Sherman Alexie helped create buzz for his work through public readings. He had seen other authors bomb in front of audiences by reading in a boring monotone. Alexie vowed instead to find a way to excite readers who came out to see him.

At his first reading at Elliot Bay Book Company in Seattle, he arrived just before the event was to begin. He sat in the back of the room, dressed in an old coat and holding what looked like a bottle of alcohol in a paper bag. As he recounted in a *Ploughshares* interview in 2000, he suddenly yelled out, "Where's that IN-jun poet?" and stumbled toward the podium up front. The audience was confused, unsure of what was going on, when he stripped off his costume and began to recite his poetry from memory.

To his surprise, Alexie proved a natural performer. As he recalled in a video broadcast on BigThink.com, "I got on stage, and started talking and people laughed. In the beginning, I didn't even necessarily know what was happening." He had never thought of himself as funny before he started performing his work in front of an audience. In the Big Think video, Alexie credited the example of his brothers and sisters as inspiring his wit in public appearances: "I never really was the funny guy growing up. You can ask my siblings. They'd tell you I was the depressed guy in the basement. They're the funny ones."

BUILDING A CAREER

Established as a rising star in American poetry, Alexie continued to write at a rapid pace. Between 1992 and 1996, he published seven collections of poems, including *First Indian on the Moon* (1993), *Old Shirts and New Skins* (1993), *Seven Mourning Songs for the Cedar Flute I Have Yet to Learn to Play* (1994), *The Summer of Black Widows* (1996), and *Water Flowing Home* (1996).

During this time, Alexie married Diane Tomhave, whom he met while judging a writing contest at a camp for American Indian children where she was employed. Tomhave is of Hidatsa, Ho-Chunk, and Potawatomi Indian heritage. In an interview with the *Guardian* in 2008, Alexie explained why he had wanted to marry a fellow Indian: "My wife was the first romantic partner who understood both American and native parts of me—not so much the positive stuff, but the damage." Since their marriage in 1995, the couple has had two sons, Joseph and David.

Despite his success as a poet, Alexie made a decision to take his writing career in a new direction. The readership for poetry is small, and Alexie wanted to write for a larger audience. With that in mind, he began writing prose in addition to poetry.

SINGING THE RESERVATION BLUES

At the beginning of each chapter in his novel *Reservation Blues*, Sherman Alexie included a selection of lyrics, supposedly the work of a fictional band named Coyote Springs. In 1995, Alexie worked with the Colville Indian singer Jim Boyd to put these words to music. The result was *Reservation Blues: The Soundtrack*. On the CD, Boyd sings and plays guitar while Alexie performs his lyrics in a voice-over. Alexie has since produced another soundtrack featuring songs from *The Business of Fancydancing*, the 2002 feature film that he wrote and directed.

LONE RANGER AND RESERVATION BLUES

Alexie's first work of fiction is a collection of short stories titled *The Lone Ranger and Tonto Fistfight in Heaven* (1993). The book introduces two characters who reappear in his later works. Victor Joseph is a former athlete struggling to come to terms with his Indian heritage. His friend, the nerdy Thomas Builds-the-Fire, is a natural storyteller. Alexie has explained that both Victor and Thomas grew out of different aspects of himself. Another critical success, *Lone*

In his fiction, Alexie often features real historical figures as characters. For instance, the blues legend Robert Johnson makes an appearance on the Spokane Indian Reservation in Alexie's novel *Reservation Blues*.

Ranger was a finalist for the 1993 PEN/Hemingway Award for the year's best first work of fiction.

After *Lone Ranger*, Alexie felt ready to take on still another literary form—the novel. Like *Lone Ranger*, the sprawling *Reservation Blues* is initially set on the Spokane reservation. Looking for spiritual guidance, the famous blues musician Robert Johnson comes to the reservation and gives his guitar to Thomas Builds-the-Fire. (The appearance of Johnson in *Reservation Blues* is an early example of one of Alexie's favorite literary devices: the introduction of real-life people into his fictional narratives.) With the guitar in hand, Thomas and Victor start up an all-Indian rock band called Coyote Springs, which attracts the attention of record executives wanting to use their Indian background as a marketing hook.

The novel explores the struggles of Indians, particularly Indian artists, to find their place in a society that is often hostile to them. *Reservation Blues* was widely praised and received the Before Columbus Foundation's American Book Award in 1996. With its publication, Alexie established himself as an up-and-coming novelist as well as a respected short story writer and heralded poet—all at the age of twenty-seven.

FINDING SUCCESS

Alexie's second novel, *Indian Killer* (1996), proved to be his most controversial work yet. The book mimics the form of a murder mystery. But unlike conventional mysteries, instead of narrowing down the suspects to solve the murder, it introduces even more possible murderers as the narrative moves along. The plot focuses on a series of murders in the Seattle area. All the victims are white men. The killer scalps the victims and leaves feathers by their corpses. A right-wing radio host sensationalizes the serial murders by labeling the perpetrator as the "Indian Killer." The book explores racial tensions that explode in the wake of the unsolved killings.

Indian Killer drew mixed reviews. While some critics admired the work, others felt the white characters were drawn too broadly. Still others complained that the book was too angry. *TIME* magazine, for example, claimed Alexie was "septic with his own unappeasable anger." Alexie was so amused by the comment that he took to wearing a T-shirt emblazoned with the quote. As he explained to *Writer* magazine, "It was intentionally an angry novel. I got tired of being accused of being so angry all the time. Well, if you want to see angry, here it is."

Alexie has since come to see *Indian Killer* as his least successful work. In the *Guardian* in 2008, he dismissed it as a "product of youthful rage" whose violence he now views with "overwhelming disgust." But, according to a 2003 *Guardian* interview, the book and its themes still continue to haunt him: "It's sold by far the least of all my books. Indians didn't like it. It was the book that was hardest to write, that gave me the most nightmares, that still, to this day, troubles me the most because I can't even get a grasp on it. It's the only one I re-read. I think a book that disturbs me that much is the one I probably care the most about."

SMOKE SIGNALS

After the publication of *Indian Killer*, Alexie decided to shift gears again. He began writing a screenplay based on material from *The Lone Ranger and Tonto*

Fistfight in Heaven, drawing especially on the story "This Is What It Means to Say Phoenix, Arizona." Alexie wanted to tap into the storytelling power of film, as well as capture a larger audience for

Alexie *(right)* wrote the screenplay for the film *Smoke Signals* (1998), which Chris Eyre *(left)* directed. *Smoke Signals* is thought to be the first movie written, directed, and produced by American Indians.

his work—one that would include more American Indians. As he explained to *Ploughshares* in 2000: "I…became increasingly aware that my audience was made up of white faces. It bugged me that there weren't more brown faces. Then I realized that books weren't going to do it. I needed to broaden things, working in art forms that were more accessible to Indians."

Alexie first prepared by reading books about screenwriting, but soon realized they were not teaching him much. In a *Writer* magazine interview, he remembered thinking, "I'm a writer. Putting words on paper, that's what I do." He instead began watching lots of movies to better understand the form and then began writing.

The result was the screenplay for *Smoke Signals* (1998), which Alexie also coproduced. Although there had previously been films about contemporary Indians, Alexie's movie is considered the first written, directed, and produced by American Indians. It was the first feature directed by Chris Eyre, the Arapaho/Cheyenne director whose later films included *Skins* (2002) and *Edge of America* (2003).

MODERN INDIANS ON FILM

Alexie was adamant that American Indian actors be cast in all the lead roles. As he said in the 1998 *New York Times* article "An Indian Without Reservations,"

Adam Beach, Irene Bedard, and Evan Adams pose at the premiere of *Smoke Signals*. Unlike most Hollywood fare, Indian actors played all the American Indian characters in the film.

he wanted "[n]o Italians with long hair," mocking the long-standing Hollywood traditions of casting white people in Indian parts. *Smoke Signals* starred Adam Beach, a young Ojibwa Indian actor from Canada, as Victor Joseph. The plot revolves around Victor's trip from his Idaho reservation to Phoenix, Arizona, to collect the ashes of his late father. He is accompanied by Thomas Builds-the-Fire, who is played by Coast Salish actor Evan Adams.

Alexie wanted to tell a contemporary story in his first movie as an anecdote to how Indians had been portrayed in films in the past. In old westerns, as well as in many recent films, Indians were usually either warriors or shamans, holy men who helped spiritually heal or enlighten other, mostly white, characters. (*Smoke Signals* openly mocked these Hollywood stereotypes. At one point, Thomas, while watching television, jokes, "The only thing more pathetic than Indians on TV is Indians watching Indians on TV.") In contrast, *Smoke Signals* tells the story of everyday people with everyday problems. It also attempts to paint a realistic and unsentimental picture of how many contemporary Indians live now.

Smoke Signals premiered at the prestigious Sundance Film Festival. There, it won two awards— the Filmmaker Trophy (Drama) and the Audience Award (Drama), the latter given to the dramatic film audiences named as their favorite in the festival.

Smoke Signals also was named Best Film at the 1998 American Indian Film Festival. The movie earned almost $7 million, which, for an independent film at the time, was an impressive box-office take.

STRUGGLING WITH THE MOVIE INDUSTRY

Alexie hoped that the success of *Smoke Signals* would inspire other Indians to carve out careers in film. "These 13-year-old Indian kids who've been going crazy with their camcorders will finally see the possibilities," Alexie predicted in a 1998 interview with *Time*. He also began to pursue other film projects for himself. He set to work on movie adaptations of *Reservation Blues* and *Indian Killer,* as well as a screenplay based on *Young Men and Fire*, a novel by Norman MacLean.

But despite the success of *Smoke Signals*, Alexie had trouble getting any of these films off the ground. He became frustrated dealing with Hollywood executives and the slow progress he was making. In 2000, he told the literary journal *Ploughshares*, "The movie world is fine, but I really grew disillusioned with it in many ways...[S]o much has to happen for a movie to get made." In contrast to his struggles with the film industry, Alexie came to appreciate the creative satisfaction he found in the publishing

Sherman Alexie *(second from the right)* and *The Business of Fancydancing* stars Gene Tagaban, Evan Adams, and Michelle St. John attended the screening of the film at the Sundance Film Festival in 2002. *Fancydancing* was Alexie's directorial debut.

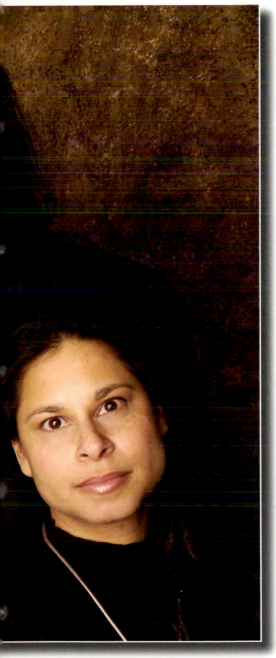

world. As he explained to *Ploughshares*, "I write a book, and it gets published. I like the immediacy of it. I'd forgotten what it meant to be a writer. As much as people love movies, they really hold authors in high esteem. It's one thing to make a movie and quite another when people want to hear your voice."

Alexie did get one other movie project made—a film version of *The Business of Fancydancing* (2002), which he both wrote and directed. The film is told from the perspective of Seymour Polatkin, a gay Indian writer who returns to his reservation after years of being away to attend the funeral of a high school

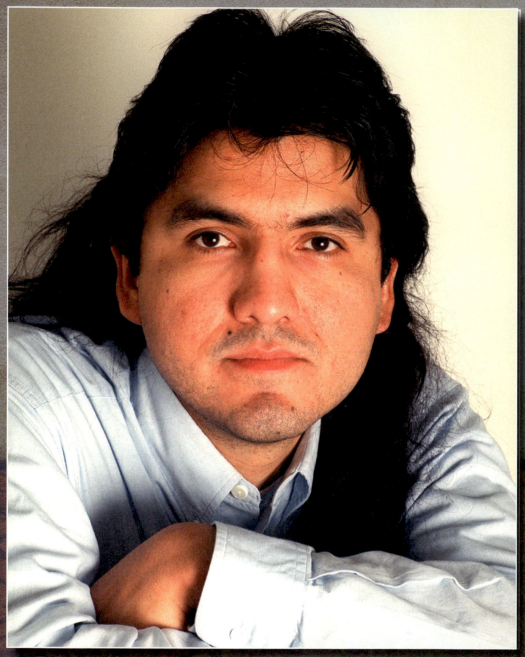

Alexie turned to filmmaking in the hope of attracting a new audience, one that would include other American Indians. "I needed to broaden things," he explained, "working in art forms that were more accessible to Indians."

friend. Shot in an experimental style on a very low budget, the movie failed to find an audience.

WRITER'S BLOCK

Alexie's adventures in the film industry had an unwelcome effect on his writing. For the first time in his career, he had had dozens of people—directors, producers, and film executives—constantly evaluating his work, offering their own, often conflicting, suggestions for rewrites and changes. He described in an interview published on OregonLive.com the stress of having "[t]wenty different people saying 20 different things, and all of them questioning your ability": "At first I was just hearing those voices when I was writing on screenplays but then they started intruding, creeping into my head and everything else I was writing. When you start hearing some surrogate producer when you're working on a poem, nothing happens. I think my imagination deflated."

In the past, Alexie had been incredibly prolific, often going on writing binges during which the words just seemed to pour out of him. Suddenly, he found himself with a crippling case of writer's block. No matter how hard he tried, he was unable to write anything for much of 1999 and 2000. The experience both panicked and depressed him. As he told OregonLive.com, "I started consoling

In 1999 and 2000, Alexie feared his literary career was over when he suffered a severe case of writer's block. But once he began writing again, he entered one of his most prolific periods, which saw the publication of volumes of poetry, short story collections, and novels.

myself with the thought that if nothing else ever happens I've had an incredible career. I guess it was sort of sad, too. I'm thinking, 'I'm a young man. What am I going to do?'"

It ended up taking another artist to free Alexie from his writer's block. While visiting the author David James Duncan in Montana, he toured the studio of Duncan's wife, a ceramic sculptor named Adrian Arleo. Alexie was admiring her work when the first lines of a poem popped into his head. That night, he wrote two poems, the first he had set down in many months.

RETURNING TO LITERATURE

The block was gone, and Alexie returned to writing at his customarily frenetic pace. In 2000, he published a new book of poems, *One Stick Song*. Alexie's later poetry collections include *Dangerous Astronomy* (2005) and *Face* (2009).

Alexie returned to the short story in the acclaimed *Toughest Indian in the World* (2000). In this volume, Alexie focused his attention largely on the lives and struggles of urban Indians—that is, Indians who live in cities rather than rural areas, where most reservations are located. Alexie wanted to write about urban Indians because they make up about three-fourths of the American Indian population, but many contemporary Indian authors ignore their stories. On Atlantic.com in 2000, Alexie explained that "the ironic thing is very, very few of those we call Native American writers actually grew up on reservations, and yet most of their work is about reservations. As someone who grew up on a reservation, I'm tired of it. No, I'm exhausted." His 2003 story collection *Ten Little Indians* similarly explores urban themes. Most of its stories are about Spokane Indians living in Seattle.

In 2007, Alexie published *Flight*, his first novel in ten years. It tells the story of Zits, a half-Indian fifteen-year-old boy stuck in the foster care system. The narrative follows Zits as his soul flies into bodies of other people during various times in history, including a witness to the Battle of Little Bighorn in

1876 and a racist FBI agent on an Indian reservation in the 1970s. By placing his protagonist in different bodies, Alexie explores America's history of racial violence from both a white and Indian perspective.

Because of Zits' age, some critics mistook *Flight* as a book for young readers. To Alexie, though, the book's violent content made it firmly an adult novel. But, in his fiction, Alexie would soon return to exploring the world through the eyes of a young character. That next work would prove to be the greatest success in Alexie's already extraordinary career.

WRITING FOR YOUNG READERS

Always eager to experiment with new genres, Alexie set out to write his first nonfiction book. It was going to be a history of his family, emphasizing his father's and grandfather's experiences in war. He completed a big section, some 450 pages, before he realized he was losing focus. That section was all about his first year in high school in the off-reservation town in Reardan, Washington. He liked what he had written, but it did not seem to fit with his plan for the book.

While he was struggling through the manuscript, a children's book editor he was acquainted with happened to call him. Her call was not completely unexpected. About every six months, he heard from her and she always asked the same question:

When was he going to write a novel for young readers? Alexie had heard the question from plenty of other people as well. Wherever he went to give talks or read his work, teachers approached him, hoping to convince him to write something their students could enjoy.

During the call, Alexie scanned his desk and spotted the pages from his family history. Suddenly, he had an idea. As he recounted in an interview with *School Library Journal*, "I was looking at my desktop and there was the manuscript, sitting there, and I thought, 'Wow! I think that's a novel.'" He began reworking his manuscript, transforming his own story to that of a new fictional creation, fourteen-year-old Arnold Spirit Jr. The result was his first young adult novel, *The Absolutely True Diary of a Part-Time Indian* (2007).

TELLING ARNOLD'S STORY

Arnold's "absolutely true" diary is largely inspired by Alexie's own experiences when he was fourteen. To him, the subject matter was rich. As Alexie explained to SouthCoastToday.com, "[A]s I got older, I realized that was an epic year in my life. It took me 25 years to realize how amazing that year was." In some ways, he decided, it seemed too amazing to recount that year in a work of nonfiction. "[P]artly I made it a novel simply because—this is weird to say—nobody would actually believe it as a memoir," Alexie told *School Library Journal*. Most of the characters are fictional, but *True Diary* does draw largely from real events. In a speech reprinted in the *Horn Book Magazine*, Alexie explained, "[Y]es, the book is autobiographical. The book is my story. If I were to guess at the percentage, it would be about seventy-eight percent true."

Just as Alexie did, Arnold grows up on the Spokane reservation. Reservation life is portrayed as bleak, full of alcoholism, poverty, and despair. Arnold also suffers from physical problems, like Alexie had, as a result of being born with hydrocephalus. Sporting thick glasses and speaking with a lisp, Arnold is a favorite target of reservation bullies. He documents his various frustrations and humiliations in cartoons. ("Arnold's" cartoons in the book were drawn by Ellen Forney, a Seattle-based illustrator and cartoonist.)

He decides to change his life after, in a fit of fury, he throws his math book, which accidentally hits his teacher. With Arnold facing expulsion, the teacher gives him a piece of advice: Get off the reservation. As Alexie did, Arnold enrolls in a white high school just outside of the reservation borders. The rest of the novel recounts how Arnold adjusts to his new surroundings, while encountering hostility from his Indian friends and neighbors, who feel betrayed by his decision to leave the reservation school.

Alexie knew that the people and problems he depicted in *True Diary* would be very unfamiliar to most of his readers. But, he recognized that, even if they had never seen a reservation or personally known an Indian, young people could identify with Arnold and his journey. As Alexie explained on the radio show *Morning Edition*: "[W]hat [it]…come[s] down to is the search for identity. And as a teenager, everybody's going through that trying to figure out who you are."

EXPLORING YA

Because *True Diary* was so autobiographical, Alexie found it difficult to write. Revisiting his adolescence meant reliving some of his most painful memories. For instance, Arnold's sister dies in a trailer fire, just as Alexie's sister had, forcing him to recall his intense feelings of grief and mourning.

Alexie also struggled with the unfamiliar genre of young adult, or YA, fiction. Before delving into the manuscript, he thoroughly researched the field. As he told the *New York Times* in 2009, "I did a study of YA novels when I was figuring mine out—I read hundreds of them."

Even as he got a handle on the genre, he found himself overthinking what was appropriate for the

BANNING *TRUE DIARY*

In 2011, the American Library Association announced its list of the year's most frequently challenged books—that is, books that parents wanted to ban from classrooms or school libraries. *The Absolutely True Diary of a Part-Time Indian* had the dubious honor of ranking number two.

Since its publication, *True Diary* has come under attack for a variety of reasons. Some complain about the sexual subjects it takes on. Others feel that its frank depiction of poverty, racism, and alcoholism makes it inappropriate for young readers.

In an interview with MotherJones.com, Sherman Alexie claimed that when *True Diary* is banned by a school district, "[i]t means I did something right." He feels strongly that books for young people should deal with the realities they face, no matter how upsetting or dark. As he explained to SouthCoastToday. com, "There's nothing in the books that middle school kids don't deal with on a daily basis. [Banning books] happens in communities where kids are overprotected. Compared to the lives that some kids deal with, *[True Diary]* is a cakewalk."

young audience he wanted to reach. He feared that many parents, teachers, and libraries would object to his grim depiction of poverty, alcoholism, and racism—even though these issues had all been something he dealt with on a daily basis when he was the age of his readers. At one point, he decided to tone down the material. "I took out some stuff," he explained in 2011 to MotherJones.com, "but then my editor made me put it back in. It's realism."

A BEST-SELLING AUTHOR

It was just that realism, combined with Alexie's sense of humor, that made *True Diary* a favorite with critics. Many reviewers were also won over by the character of Arnold. For instance, Bruce Barcott of the *New York Times* wrote, "Working in the voice of a 14-year-old forces Alexie to strip everything down to action and emotion, so that reading becomes more like listening to your smart, funny best friend recount his day while waiting after school for a ride home." Alexie's novel won a host of prizes, including the *Boston Globe*-Horn Book Award and the National Book Award for Young People's Literature.

True Diary was not just a critical triumph. It was also an enormously popular success. It became a national best seller, which surprised Alexie as much as it delighted him. "I knew it would do well, but nobody predicts that well," Alexie explained to SouthCoastToday.com. "It's funny because at any given point on the best-sellers list, it will be vampires, magicians, dragons and me. It's surprising—not strictly because it's about an Indian kid—but because of the kind of book it is."

Sherman Alexie *(second from right)* is all smiles as he shows off his National Book Award and the novel that won it for him. He stands with fellow winners Robert Hass and Tim Weiner and with Cindy Johnson, who accepted the award for her husband, Denis Johnson.

As Alexie traveled around the United States for personal appearances in schools, he discovered that Arnold had struck a chord with teenagers from all backgrounds. In an essay for *Publishers Weekly* in 2008, he wrote, "[R]ich kids did care about my story. So did inner-city kids in San Francisco, middle-class kids in the Chicago suburbs, and kids from the reservation, barrio, farm town and every other region of the country." In the article, Alexie came to his own conclusion about *True Diary*'s appeal to the young reading public: "Why have teens so embraced my book? I think it's because teenagers, of every class, color and creed, feel trapped by family, community and tribal expectations. And teenagers have to make the outrageous and heroic decision to re-create themselves."

AFTER *TRUE DIARY*

Several filmmakers have tried to buy the movie rights to the book. But Alexie has so far declined all offers. In an interview with the *New York Times* in 2009, he jokingly explained, "My concern was that they would never have been able to find an Indian kid who could act well enough and who was a good enough basketball player to play me."

Alexie did, however, agree to write a sequel to *True Diary*, titled *The Magic and Tragic Year of My Broken Thumb*. Alexie has reported that the new book will deal with Arnold's sophomore year in high school and involve a romance with Penelope, Arnold's love interest in *True Diary*. To work on the sequel, Alexie had to stop writing *Radioactive Love Song*, another YA manuscript he was working on. He, however, was happy to have an excuse to put it aside. As he explained in an interview at failbetter. com, "Arnold kept talking to me. He wouldn't let me write the other book, he wouldn't let me finish it. He kept getting in the way of the other book."

Arnold's voice did subside enough to allow Alexie to write two new books for adults. Published in 2009, *Face* is a poetry collection in which he plays with several classic forms, such as the sonnet and the villanelle. Appearing in the same year, *War Dances* is a combination of short fiction and

Alexie reads from his book *Ten Little Indians* at a New York City bookstore in 2011. Unlike many authors, he enjoys making public appearances and speaking with devoted readers.

poems. In his SouthCoastToday.com interview, Alexie noted that the book was a departure for him because, instead of focusing on Indian identity, it dealt with the more universal subject of "[m]en and their failure."

After the blockbuster success of *True Diary*, Alexie embraced the chance to return to small press publishing with *War Dances*. As he explained in a 2010 article in the *New York Times*, "I think the new book was an attempt to re-establish my eccentric self: 'I'm not supposed to sell as many copies as I just did, so let me write something that won't.'" Although it did not sell anywhere near as well as *True Diary*, *War Dances* received good reviews. It also won the prestigious PEN/Faulkner Foundation Award for fiction.

YOUNG READERS' "CRAZIEST ALLY"

The publication of *True Diary* brought Alexie worldwide attention and made him financially secure. But, on a personal level, it helped him understand and come to terms with his often difficult childhood. In a speech at an awards ceremony held by *Horn Book Magazine*, he explained, "That's one of the amazing things about the acceptance of the book because in really large ways it feels like my story, my choices, have been validated by this huge group of people."

Just as important to Alexie, it also allowed him to connect with an entirely new audience. From readers' responses, Alexie explained at the *Horn Book* ceremony, he learned "that pretty much every teenager out there, regardless of class or race or culture or geography, feels pretty dang isolated and pretty dang misunderstood." Alexie was pleased to discover that these readers are inspired by Arnold and his life-changing decision to explore the world outside his reservation. As Alexie put it to his audience, "I think that's a lot of what teenagers have responded to: they see in a book that you can make your own decisions for yourself and still be a loving member of your family and your community."

Such responses have encouraged Alexie in his new and latest career as a young adult novelist. "I write because I know there is a kid out there who needs my book," Alexie explained in *Publishers Weekly*. "There might be one thousand, one hundred thousand or one million such kids. I want to be their favorite writer, craziest ally and honored guest."

FIVE

CHAPTER

TELLING STORIES

Sherman Alexie is a born storyteller. As soon as he set his sights on a literary career, he began writing at a furious pace. Aside from a brief, unsettling bout of writer's block, he has continued to publish book after book for more than twenty years.

But, as Alexie explains, even though he is prolific, writing is often far from easy for him. He works at it each day and often well into the night, when his insomnia leaves him restless. As Alexie told *Ploughshares*, as a writer "[y]ou can't get lazy. I'm doing something around it every day—reading, writing, editing, thinking. I can be staring out the window, and I'm working real hard."

A PROFESSIONAL WRITER

In his *Ploughshares* interview, he described himself as a "binge writer." He might write as much as 150 pages in just a few days. But often a writing binge does not yield as much publishable work as he hopes. As he explained to the *New York Times* in 2009, out of that 150 pages, "maybe I'll scrap it all because it's terrible, or it'll become four lines of a poem."

Alexie is far more critical of his work than his fans and even most reviewers. "I work on probably about a 2 percent greatness rate," he explained in a video on BigThink.com. "So there's probably 10 poems, 2 stories that are great. And the rest of it is anywhere from pretty good to total crap."

From the start, Alexie has always been serious about his career, noting that writing is not just an art, but also a business. In a *Writer* magazine interview, he said that, as a professional writer, he is always working to turn a profit: "My publishers pay me a lot of money to write books. I'm going to do all I can to help them get that money back."

This sense of professionalism was one reason why he has chosen to explore so many different genres. He admits, though, freed of any financial concerns, he would write only poetry. But he turned to fiction because it was a way to find a larger

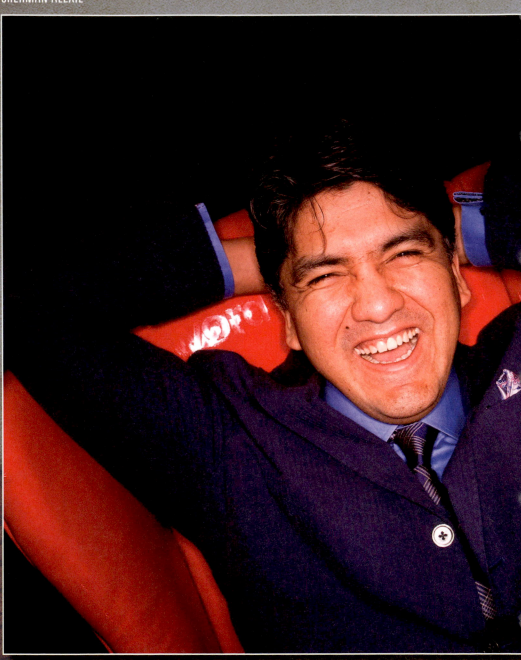

Throughout his career, Sherman Alexie has been amazingly prolific. Although he often writes quickly, he still considers it hard work. As he has explained about writing fiction, in an interview on failbetter.com, "It's a great job, I love my job, but it's a job."

audience. As he put it to failbetter.com, "[P]oetry is the thing I love to do most, and writing fiction is my job. It's a great job, I love my job, but it's a job. Writing poetry's not a job, it doesn't feel that way at all."

INDIANS IN REAL LIFE

Both through his fiction and his poetry, Alexie throughout his career has dealt with American Indian life in the modern world. In Alexie's eyes, the subject is extraordinarily rich. As he explained to *Writer*, "Every theme, every story, every tragedy that exists in literature takes place in my little community. *Hamlet* takes place on my reservation daily. *King Lear* takes place on my reservation daily. It's a powerful place. I'm never going to run out of stories."

Writing about reservation life has also helped broaden his audience. In 1996, *Granta* magazine in the United Kingdom named Alexie one of the best twenty American novelists under the age of forty. Speaking to the *Guardian* in 2003, *Granta* editor Ian Jack speculated that Alexie's favorite subject was part of the reason for his selection: "I can't speak for my fellow jurists, but I suspect that they, like me, liked his work because it had something to tell us. Native American life, life on the reservation, is a pretty under-described experience. I knew nothing about it…Alexie told me

about things I hadn't thought of before, this must also be true of many people in the USA."

A sign on the entrance to the Pine Ridge Indian Reservation in South Dakota warns that alcohol is not permitted within its borders. In much of his work, Alexie explores the destruction and despair resulting from alcohol abuse in many American Indian communities.

Alexie was not the first American Indian novelist to write about contemporary Indian life. Before he began his career, Indian writers such as N. Scott Momaday, Leslie Silko, and Louise Erdrich had won awards and accolades for their takes on the subject. Alexie, however, distinguished himself for his willingness to show the harsh realities of reservation life, no matter how poorly it might reflect on his people. He has often been criticized for his depiction of widespread alcoholism on the Spokane reservation, which some critics believe serves to reinforce the old stereotype of the "drunken Indian." In *Writer* magazine, Alexie defended his depiction of the problem among the Spokane: "I would say no sober Indian has ever objected to the way I have written about life on the reservation. I write about alcoholics because I am a recovering alcoholic. If I extend my family out as far as I possibly can to include a hundred or more people—all but maybe two of them are alcoholics."

Alexie still regularly visits the reservation to see family and friends. His mother and siblings also often attend readings that he gives in the city of Spokane, Washington. But, as he freely admits, not all his fellow tribespeople are as supportive of his success. In 1998, when *New York Times* reporter Timothy Egan visited the Spokane Indian

Reservation, several residents offered blunt criticisms of Alexie and his work. For instance, tribal college librarian Mikki Samuels said, "What people on the reservation feel is that he's making fun of them. It's supposed to be fiction, but we all know who he's writing about. He has wounded a lot of people. And a lot of people feel he should try to write something positive."

SPEAKING OUT

Writing with candor and passion about Indian issues has not only caused tensions between him and some other Indian writers and readers. It has also made him something of an unofficial spokesperson in the press for American Indians everywhere—a position Alexie does not always appreciate. But it is not surprising given that, since the publication of *True Diary*, he has become probably the most famous American Indian writer working today.

Alexie recognizes that this alone gives him what, in a 2003 *Guardian* interview, he called "enormous cultural power." He also acknowledges that his role as a public figure helps promote a positive image of Indian people. In 1998, he explained to the *New York Times*, "I'm sober. I'm married to an Indian woman. I have a stable family life. I'm polite. I've become a good role model."

In his public appearances and in his writing, Alexie has worked to counter stereotypes about Indians, both good and bad. For instance, he joked to LovetheBook.com that, despite his down-to-earth demeanor "people assume I have all these magical Indian powers, like I'm some sort of healer or shaman." Alexie especially likes to mock non-Indian wannabes who embrace so-called Indian spirituality. In a 1998 *New York Times* article, he asked, "[W]hat's with all these sensitive New Age guys beating drums in the woods, trying to be Indians? Hey, Indians gave that up a hundred years ago. Now we're sitting on the couch with the remote." Alexie is also critical of non-Indians who write in the voice of Indian characters because they believe they understand how it feels to be Indian. As he explained to the *Guardian*, "I don't care what people write about, but I get distressed when people so identify [with Indians] that they think they become something they're not."

Alexie also has taken some fellow Indian writers to task for writing only about reservation Indians. He complains that most, unlike him, did not grow up on a reservation, so they are often not writing from experience. Alexie also feels their focus leaves urban Indians, who now make up the majority of the American Indian population in the United States, all but unseen in literature.

HEAVYWEIGHT POETRY

Throughout his career, Sherman Alexie has earned many honors. Perhaps the oddest is the title Heavyweight Poetry Champion of the World. He won the title four times at the Taos Poetry Circus, which was held in Taos, New Mexico, for eighteen years. The event was meant to showcase contemporary poets and build an enthusiastic audience for their work.

During each of the ten rounds of the World Poetry Bout, two poets read one of their works. The poet scored highest by a team of judges advanced to the next round. The last two poets standing competed in the final round to determine who would become the Heavyweight Poetry Champion.

Sherman Alexie competed in the bout in 1998, 1999, 2000, and 2001. He was named champion each time. Nicknamed the "Sherminator," Alexie retired.

MAKING FUN

Alexie holds that he is unique among American Indian writers in his embrace of popular culture. When he cites his major influences, he often names the classic novel *The Grapes of Wrath* (1939) by John Steinbeck. But just as frequently he will list the horror writer Stephen King; the 1960s sitcom *The Brady Bunch*; or the game of basketball, which he

Sherman Alexie amuses host Craig Ferguson during the filming of *The Late Late Show* in 2007. Because of his quick wit, Alexie has frequently been invited to appear on television talk shows.

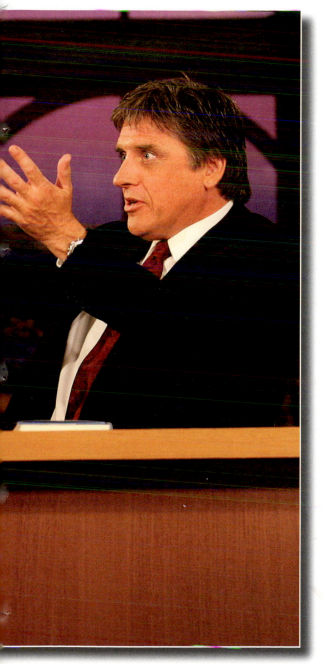

still plays to clear his mind between writing sessions. Like most Americans, his characters, too, have their pop culture obsessions. For instance, in *Reservation Blues*, the greatest ambition of the all-Indian band Coyote Springs is to become the opening act for the rock supergroup Aerosmith.

Another common element in Alexie's work is humor. He is known for his witty take on even the most difficult subjects. In the journal *MELUS*, Alexie complained that "[p]eople assume that you're not being serious because you're being funny," while at the same time realizing he has no choice but to write with a humorous slant: "[B]eing funny is just how I am. I can't just stop."

At the same time, he recognizes the power of humor to bring people together. As he explained in a BigThink.com video, "Humor is pretty amazing in its ability to transcend differences—politically, ethnically, racially, geographically, economically. There's something about it that really opens people up spiritually, I think. And they listen, they pay attention."

AROUND THE FIRE

Over the past twenty years, Alexie has become an internationally acclaimed writer. At the same time, he has amassed a collection of many of the most prestigious literary awards. And with the publication of *True Diary*, Alexie also established himself as a presence on best-seller lists, a feat he is bound to repeat in young adult literature and perhaps other genres in the years to come.

Alexie's success, however, did not come easily. Not only did he have to commit himself to working hard on his writing every day. He also made it a point to meet his readers and perform his stories for them. In this way, his work hearkens back to that of his material grandmother, who was known among the Spokane as a great teller of tales. Like other Indian groups, the Spokane have a long tradition of

Alexie's short story collection *Ten Little Indians*, published in 2003, returned to one of his favorite themes—the struggles of urban American Indians in contemporary society. Critics and reviewers alike consider Alexie an accomplished poet and storyteller.

elders entertaining and instructing young tribe members with stories, often as they gathered around a raging fire.

Alexie himself drew that parallel in a video on BigThink.com: "I made a career out of traveling from bookstore to bookstore, university [to] university, audience member to audience member, and talking to them about my book, and reading from my book, and performing my book. I was doing something old-fashioned. I was a storyteller around a fire."

FACT SHEET ON SHERMAN ALEXIE

Birth date: October 7, 1966

Birthplace: Spokane, Washington

Colleges attended: Gonzaga University in Spokane; Washington State University in Pullman

Degrees: Bachelor of arts in American studies from Washington State University, Pullman in 1994

Current residence: Seattle, Washington

Occupation: Full-time writer

Marital status: Married to Diane Tomhave in 1995

Children: Joseph and David

First book: *The Business of Fancydancing* (poetry collection, 1992)

Major works: *Reservation Blues* (novel, 1995), *Indian Killer* (novel, 1996), *The Lone Ranger and Tonto Fistfight in Heaven* (short story collection, 1993), *Smoke Signals* (screenplay, 1998), *The Toughest Indian in the World* (short story collection, 2000), *The Absolutely True Diary of a Part-Time Indian* (young adult novel, 2007), *War Dances* (short story collection, 2009)

Awards and honors: (see "Fact Sheet on Sherman Alexie's Work" for awards given for specific books): Washington State Arts Commission Poetry Fellowship (1991), the National Endowment for the Arts Poetry Fellowship (1992), Lila Wallace/Readers' Digest Writer's Award (1994), Granta's Twenty Best American Novelists Under the Age of

40 (1996), World Heavyweight Championship Poetry Bout at the Taos Poetry Circus (1998, 1999, 2000, 2001), *New Yorker*'s 20 Writers for the 21st Century (1999), PEN/Malamund Award (2001), Washington State University Regents' Distinguished Alumnus (2003), Stranger Genius Award (2008), Mason Award (2009), Native Writers' Circle of the Americas Lifetime Achievement Award (2010), Puterbaugh Fellow (2010)

ON SHERMAN ALEXIE'S WORK

YOUNG ADULT NOVELS

The Absolutely True Diary of a Part-Time Indian.
Boston, MA: Little, Brown, 2007.

Synopsis: In this autobiographical young adult novel, fourteen-year-old Arnold Spirit Jr. wants relief from the poverty and despair of the Indian reservation where he was raised. He decides to do what no Indian he knows has ever done—transfer to an off-reservation white-dominated school where he can get a better education and possibly a better life.

Awards: National Book Award for Young People's Literature (2007), *Los Angeles Times* Book Prize (finalist, 2007), American Indian Youth Literature Award (2008), *Boston Globe*-Horn Book Award (2008), Scandiuzzi Children's Book Award (2008), Peter Pan Prize (2009), California Young Reader Medal (2010)

Translations: Dutch, French, German, Japanese, Spanish, and Swedish

ADULT NOVELS

Reservation Blues. New York, NY: Warner Books, 1995.

Synopsis: Given a guitar by blues legend Robert Johnson, Thomas Builds-the-Fire and his friend Victor Joseph form an all-Indian rock band, Coyote Springs. With characteristic humor, Alexie takes his characters on a journey from the reservation to the big city in this comic story about redemption.
Awards: Before Columbus Foundation's American Book Award (1996), Murray Morgan Prize (1995)
Translations: French, German

Indian Killer. New York, NY: Warner Books, 1996.
Synopsis: Racial tensions in Seattle, Washington, reach a boiling point when a serial killer, dubbed the "Indian Killer" by the media, begins targeting white men. In this unconventional and controversial mystery novel, Alexie examines the lives of contemporary American Indians and the rage they feel over the many injustices suffered by their peoples.
Awards: *New York Times* Book Review Notable Book (1996)
Translations: German, Spanish

Flight. New York, NY: Black Cat, 2007.
Synopsis: In this surreal novel, fifteen-year-old Zits' soul travels through time and space, inhabiting different bodies in various eras. With this literary device, Alexie examines American Indian history and issues through the eyes of Indians and non-Indians in the past and in the present.
Translations: French

SHORT STORY COLLECTIONS

The Lone Ranger and Tonto Fistfight in Heaven.
New York, NY: Atlantic Monthly Press, 1993.
Awards: PEN/Hemingway Award for best fiction debut (finalist)
Translations: French, German

The Toughest Indian in the World. New York, NY: Atlantic Monthly Press, 2000.
Translations: French

Ten Little Indians. New York, NY: Grove Press, 2003.
Translations: French, Spanish

War Dances. New York, NY: Grove Press, 2009.
Translations: French

POETRY COLLECTIONS

The Business of Fancydancing: Stories and Poems. Brooklyn, NY: Hanging Loose Press, 1992.
Awards: *New York Times* Book Review Notable Book of the Year (1992)

I Would Steal Horses. Niagara Falls, NY: Slipstream Press, 1992.

First Indian on the Moon. Brooklyn, NY: Hanging Loose Press, 1993.

Old Shirts and New Skins. Los Angeles, CA: American Indian Studies Center, University of California, Los Angeles, 1993.

Seven Mourning Songs for the Cedar Flute I Have Yet to Learn to Play. Spokane, WA: Whitman College Book Arts Press, 1994.

The Summer of Black Widows. Brooklyn, NY: Hanging Loose Press, 1996.

Water Flowing Home. Boise, ID: Limberlost Press, 1996.

The Man Who Loves Salmon. Boise, ID: Limberlost Press, 1998.

One Stick Song. Brooklyn, NY: Hanging Loose Press, 2000.

Dangerous Astronomy. Boise, ID: Limberlost Press, 2005.

Face. Brooklyn, NY: Hanging Loose Press, 2009.

SCREENPLAYS

Smoke Signals: The Screenplay. New York, NY: Hyperion, 1998.

Awards (for film): Sundance Audience Award, Sundance Filmmaker Trophy

The Business of Fancydancing: The Screenplay.
Brooklyn, NY: Hanging Loose Press, 2003.

RECORDINGS

Alexie, Sherman, with Jim Boyd. *Reservation Blues: The Soundtrack.* Thunderwolf Productions, CD, 1995.

Alexie, Sherman, with others. *The Business of Fancydancing: Music from the Movie.* FallsApart Productions, CD, 2003.

The Business of Fancydancing (1992)

"Alexie writes affectingly about life on a reservation in eastern Washington State. His work displays tremendous pain and anger, but there is also love, humor, and plenty of irony."—*Library Journal*, October 1, 1992

The Lone Ranger and Tonto Fistfight in Heaven (1993)

"Alexie ruptures narratives, confuses human and fictitious people, pastiches images, and plays with illusion…The aggregative technique of writing uses many vignettes that add up to a new kind of written storytelling that comes-often-too close to the truth."—*American Indian Quarterly*, Winter 1996

Reservation Blues (1995)

"In *Reservation Blues*, Alexie…uses his own experiences growing up on the Wellpinit reservation outside Spokane as a springboard for this high-flying, humor-spiked tale of culture and assimilation…Alexie explores the place where dreams and down-and-dirty reality collide."—*People*, May 8, 1995

Indian Killer (1996)

"Alexie transforms the genre into a sharp, multilayered format that enables him to engage his readers on a number of levels…Within the highly accessible format of the thriller, Alexie has profound things to say about the identity and the plight of the American Indian."—*Christian Science Monitor*, January 6, 1997

The Absolutely True Diary of a Part-Time Indian (2007)

"Junior's narration is intensely alive and rat-a-tat-tat with short paragraphs and one liners…The dominant mode of the novel is comic, even though there's plenty of sadness…Junior's spirit, though, is unquenchable, and his style inimitable."—*Horn Book Magazine*, September/October 2007

"Jazzy syntax and Forney's witty cartoons examining Indian versus White attire and behavior transmute despair into dark humor; Alexie's no-holds-barred jokes have the effect of throwing the seriousness of his themes into high relief."
—*Publishers Weekly*, August 20, 2007

"[Arnold] weathers the typical teenage indignations and triumphs like a champ but soon faces far more trying ordeals as his home life begins to crumble and decay amidst the suffocating mire of alcoholism on the reservation…Younger teens looking for the strength to lift themselves out of rough situations would do well to start here."—*Booklist*, August 1, 2007

"Alexie nimbly blends sharp wit with unapologetic emotion in his first foray into young-adult literature… Junior's keen cartoons sprinkle the pages as his fluid narration deftly mingles raw feeling with funny, sardonic insight."—*Kirkus Reviews*, July 15, 2007

War Dances

"Alexie unfurls highly expressive language, and while at times his jokes bomb and the characters' anger can feel forced, overall this is a spiritedly provocative array of tragic comedies."—*Publishers Weekly*, August 24, 2009

TIMELINE

1966 Sherman Alexie is born on October 7 in Spokane, Washington.

1980 He begins attending Reardan High School in Reardan, Washington.

1985 Alexie begins to attend Gonzaga University.

1987 He attends Washington State University.

1990 Alexie publishes his first poems in *Hanging Loose* magazine.

1992 He publishes *The Business of Fancydancing*; *Fancydancing* is named a *New York Times Book Review* Notable Book of the Year.

1993 Alexie publishes *The Lone Ranger and Tonto Fistfight in Heaven*; it is named a finalist for the PEN/Hemingway Award for Best First Book of Fiction.

1994 He graduates from Washington State University, Pullman, with a bachelor's degree in American Studies.

1995 He publishes his first novel, *Reservation Blues*; Alexie marries Diane Tomhave.

1996 He publishes *Indian Killer*.

1998 *Smoke Signals*, a film with a screenplay by Alexie, is released and wins two awards at the Sundance Film Festival.

1999 Alexie is named one of "20 Writers for the 21st Century" by the *New Yorker*.

2001 He wins the PEN/Malamud Award for short fiction; he becomes the only poet to win the World Heavyweight Championship Poetry Bout at the Taos Poetry Circus four years in a row.

2003 *The Business of Fancydancing*, a film written and directed by Alexie, is released.

2007   He publishes *The Absolutely True Diary of a Part-Time Indian*; Alexie wins the National Book Award for Young People's Literature.

2009   He wins the PEN/Faulkner Foundation Award for Fiction for *War Dances*.

2010   Alexie wins the Native Writers' Circle of the Americas Lifetime Achievement Award; he is named the first American fellow of the Puterbaugh Foundation.

2011   The Free Library of Philadelphia selects *War Dances* and *The Absolutely True Diary of a Part-Time Indian* for its One Book, One Philadelphia citywide reading program.

ACCOLADE Praise for outstanding merit.

ADAMANT Refusing to be persuaded or to change one's mind.

ADAPTATION A stage or film version of a written work.

ALCOHOLISM A condition in which a person cannot stop drinking alcohol.

AMERICAN INDIAN A member of one of the native peoples of North and South America.

ANTHOLOGY A collection of poems or other short literary works.

BAN To prevent others' access to a book or other creative work.

BEST SELLER A book that has sold extremely well.

CANDOR Honesty.

CONTEMPORARY Occurring in or belonging to the present day.

CONTROVERSIAL Prompting extreme disagreement.

DEMEANOR Outward appearance and behavior.

EDITOR An employee of a publishing company that prepares books for publication.

EUPHORIA A feeling of intense well-being.

FANCYDANCING A fast and athletic style of dancing performed at modern Indian powwows.

FICTION Literature about made-up people and events.

FRENETIC Fast and energetic in a wild and uncontrolled way.

GENRE A category of literature in which works share a certain style and subject matter.

HYDROCEPHALUS A life-threatening condition in which fluid collects in the brain.

INSOMNIA The inability to sleep.

GLOSSARY

LITERATURE A body of written works.

MANUSCRIPT A text, usually for a book, that has not yet been published.

MEMOIR A person's written account of his or her own life.

MONOTONE A single, unvarying tone.

NARRATIVE A story.

NOVEL A book-length work of fiction.

PODIUM A stand used to hold notes when a person is delivering a speech.

POPULAR CULTURE Creative works, such as books, television shows, and movies, meant to appeal to a large audience.

POWWOW An event during which American Indians (and sometimes non-Indians) gather to enjoy Indian foods, music, and dancing.

PROFIT Money made in a business venture after subtracting expenses.

PROLIFIC Producing a large number of creative works.

PROTAGONIST The main character in a work of fiction.

RESERVATION An area of land set aside for the exclusive use of an American Indian group.

REZ A slang term for reservation.

RIGHT-WING Conservative or reactionary.

SENSATIONALIZE To create artificial excitement about something.

SEPTIC Infected.

STEREOTYPE A group of oversimplified or incorrect ideas about a particular group of people.

SURREAL Bizarre; seeming like a dream or fantasy.

SYNAPSE A junction of nerve cells.

TRIBE A group of people with a common ancestor who share cultural customs, religious beliefs, and language.

WANDERLUST A desire to travel.

WRITER'S BLOCK A condition in which a person is unable to begin or finish writing something.

YOUNG ADULT (YA) A publishing term for fiction meant to appeal to young teens.

American Indian Film Institute
333 Valencia Street, Suite 322
San Francisco, CA 94103
(415) 554-0525
Web site: http://www.aifisf.com
The American Indian Film Institute organizes the annual
 American Indian Film Festival and operates the
 Tribal Touring Program, which travels to rural reser-
 vations to teach young Indians about filmmaking.

Canadian Museum of Civilization
100 Laurier Street
Gatineau, QC K1A 0M8
Canada
(819) 776-7000
Web site: http://www.civilization.ca/cmc/home
The collections of the Museum of Civilization document
 the history and culture of North American Indians,
 with a focus on the native peoples of the Pacific
 Northwest.

Longhouse Media & Native Lens
117 East Louisa Street, #131
Seattle, WA 98102
(206) 240-5172
Web site: http://longhousemedia.org
Sherman Alexie serves on the board of directors of this
 organization, which helps young American Indian
 artists unleash their creativity with the latest media
 technologies.

National Book Foundation
90 Broad Street, Suite 604
New York, NY 10004
(212) 685-0261
Web site: http://www.nationalbook.org
This organization gives out the prestigious National
Book Awards, including one for young readers'
literature, which Sherman Alexie won in 2007. Its
Web site lists all past winners.

National Museum of the American Indian
4th Street and Independence Avenue SW
Washington, DC 20560
(202) 633-1000
Web site: http://www.nmai.si.edu
The National Museum of the American Indian, located
on the National Mall, displays exhibits about
Indian art, culture, and life in both the past and the
present.

Oyate
330 East Thomson Avenue
Sonoma, CA 95476
(707) 996-6700
Web site: http://www.oyate.org
Oyate examines children's books and other media
about Indians to determine if they represent an
Indian perspective. The organization's Web site
features recommended books and gives instruc-
tions for evaluating books about native peoples.

Seattle Indian Center
611 Twelfth Avenue South, Suite 300
Seattle, WA 98144
(206) 329-8700
Web site: http://seattleindiancenter.com
The Seattle Indian Center provides aid and services to
the city's Indian population.

Sherman Alexie Official Web Site
FallsApart Productions
PMB 2294
10002 Aurora Avenue N #36
Seattle, WA 98133
Web site: http://www.falssapart.com
This Web site is the official site for Sherman Alexie's
writing and information for fans.

SIFF Film Center
Corner of Republican and Warren Avenue N at Seattle
Center
Seattle, WA 98109
(206) 464-5830
Web site: http://www.siff.net
Sherman Alexie serves on the honorary board of the
Seattle International Film Festival (SIFF), which
sponsors the SuperFly Filmmaking Workshop for
young filmmakers.

Spokane Tribe of Indians
P.O. Box 100
Wellpinit, WA 99040

(509) 458-6500
Web site: http://spokanetribe.com
The Spokane tribe's Web site offers information and
photos about events held on its reservation in
eastern Washington State.

University of Washington Libraries
Special Collections
Allen Library South, Ground Floor
Box 352900
University of Washington
Seattle, WA 98195
(206) 685-1113
Web site: http://content.lib.washington.edu/aipnw
The University of Washington Libraries have archived a
wealth of photographs and documents concern-
ing the history of Indians in the Pacific Northwest,
much of which is available online in their digital
collections.

WEB SITES

Due to the changing nature of Internet links, Rosen
Publishing has developed an online list of Web sites
related to the subject of this book. This site is updated
regularly. Please use this link to access the list:

http://www.rosenlinks.com/AAA/Alex

"The Absolutely True Diary of a Part-Time Indian." *Horn Book Magazine*, Vol. 83, No. 5, September/October 2007, pp. 563–564.

"The Absolutely True Diary of a Part-Time Indian." *Publishers Weekly*, Vol. 254, No. 33, August 20, 2007, pp. 70–71.

Alexie, Sherman. *The Absolutely True Diary of a Part-Time Indian*. New York, NY: Little, Brown, 2007.

Alexie, Sherman. "I Still Wish." *Horn Book Magazine*, Vol. 84, No. 5, September/October 2008, p. 542.

Alexie, Sherman. "When the Story Stolen Is Your Own." *Time*, Vol. 167, No. 6, February 6, 2006, p. 72.

Barbash, Tom. "Native Son." *New York Times*, May 27, 2007.

"Big Think Interview with Sherman Alexie." BigThink.com, October 20, 2009. Retrieved August 15, 2011 (http://bigthink.com/ideas/17132).

Bruchac, Joseph. *Songs from This Earth on Turtle's Back: Contemporary American Indian Poetry*. Greenfield Center, NY: Greenfield Review Press, 1983.

Chipman, Ian. "The Absolutely True Diary of the Part-Time Indian." *Booklist*, Vol. 103, No. 22, August 1, 2007, p. 61.

Doane, Kathleen. "Sherman's March." *Cincinnati*, Vol. 40, No. 13, October 2007, p. 62.

Doherty, Craig A., and Katherine M. Doherty. *Northwest Coast Indians*. New York, NY: Chelsea House Publishers, 2010.

Frosch, Mary, ed. *Coming of Age in the 21st Century: Growing Up in America Today*. New York, NY: New Press, 2008.

Grassian, Daniel, ed. *Understanding Sherman Alexie* (Understanding Contemporary American Literature). Columbia, SC: University of South Carolina Press, 2005.

Johansen, Bruce E. *Native Americans Today: A Biographical Dictionary*. Santa Barbara, CA: Greenwood, 2010.

Kellogg, Carolyn. "Sherman Alexie—Serious Writer, Funny Guy." LATimes.com, October 16, 2009. Retrieved August 12, 2011 (http://www.latimes.com/entertainment/news/arts/la-et-sherman-alexie16-2009oct16,0,7173403.story).

King, David C. *First People: An Illustrated History of American Indians*. New York, NY: DK Publishing, 2008.

Konigsberg, Eric. "In His Own Literary World, a Native Son Without Borders." *New York Times*, October 21, 2009.

Krol, Debra Utacia. "The Absolutely True Diary of a Part-Time Indian." *Native Peoples Magazine*, Vol. 21, No. 1, January/February 2008, p. 96.

McClinton-Temple, Jennifer, and Alan Velle. *Encyclopedia of American Indian Literature*. New York, NY: Facts On File, 2007.

McKindra, Fred. "The Absolutely True Diary of a Part-Time Indian." *Entertainment Weekly*, No. 959/960, October 19, 2007, p. 131.

Nelson, Joshua B. "Humor Is My Green Card." *World Literature Today*, Vol. 84, No. 4, July/August 2010, pp. 39–43.

"Oregon High School Pulls Sherman Alexie Book from Class." Seattlepi.com, December 12, 2008.

Retrieved August 13, 2011 (http://www.seattlepi
.com/default/article/Oregon-high-school-pulls-
Sherman-Alexie-book-from-1294621.php).

Peterson, Nancy J. *Conversations with Sherman Alexie*.
Jackson, MS: University Press of Mississippi, 2009.

Purser, Heather. "Sherman Alexie, How Do You Dare to
Tell the Truth." *Yes! Magazine*, Summer 2009.
Retrieved August 12, 2011 (http://www
.yesmagazine.org/issues/the-new-economy/
sherman-alexie-how-do-you-dare-to-tell-the-truth).

Rabb, Margo. "Sherman Alexie Interview." failbetter
.com, April 21, 2009. Retrieved August 10, 2011
(http://failbetter.com/31/AlexieInterview.php?
sxnSrc=ltst).

Rich, Motoko. "Sherman Alexie Wins PEN/Faulkner
Prize." *New York Times*, March 24, 2010.

Shoemaker, Chris. "The Absolutely True Diary of a
Part-Time Indian." *School Library Journal*, Vol. 53,
No. 9, September 2007, p. 190.

Sova, Dawn B. *Literature Suppressed on Social
Grounds* (Banned Books). 3rd ed. New York, NY:
Facts On File, 2011.

Sudermann, Hannelore. "Desperately Seeking
Sherman." *Washington State Magazine*, Spring
2010. Retrieved August 10, 2011 (http://wsm.wsu
.edu/s/index.php?id=765).

Walsh, S. Kirk. "Time-Traveling Lessons for a Teenager
on the Verge." *New York Times*, April 25, 2007.

Alexie, Sherman. "Every Teen's Struggle."
PublishersWeekly.com, February 18, 2008.
Retrieved August 8, 2011 (www.publishersweekly.
com/pw/by-topic/columns-and-blogs/soapbox/
article/14017-every-teen-s-struggle-.html).

Alexie, Sherman. "Fiction and Poetry Award Winner:
The Absolutely True Diary of a Part-Time Indian."
Horn Book Magazine, January/February 2009,
Vol. 85, No. 1, pp. 25-28.

Baker, Jeff. "Native American Writer Sherman Alexie
Enjoys Being an Offensive Threat." Oregonlive
.com, October 2, 2009. Retrieved August 14,
2011 (http://www.oregonlive.com/O/index.ssf/
2009/10/post.html).

Barcott, Bruce. "Off the Rez." *New York Times*,
November 11, 2007.

Beauvais, Fred. "American Indians and Alcohol." NIAAA
.NIH.gov, 1998. Retrieved August 15, 2011 (http://
pubs.niaaa.nih.gov/publications/arh22-4/253.pdf).

Berglund, Jeff, and Jan Roush, eds. *Sherman Alexie: A
Collection of Critical Essays*. Salt Lake City, UT:
University of Utah Press, 2010.

Bruce, Heather E., et al. *Sherman Alexie in the Classroom*.
Urbana, IL.: National Council of Teachers, 2008.

Busch, Frederick. "Longing for Magic." *New York
Times*, July 16, 1995.

Butler, Kiera. "Sherman Alexie: Don't Call Me Warrior."
MotherJones.com, September 29, 2009. Retrieved
August 14, 2011 (http://motherjones.com/media/
2009/11/sherman-alexie-dont-call-me-warrior-
extended).

Campbell, Duncan. "Voice of the New Tribes." Guardian
.co.uk, January 4, 2003. Retrieved August 8,
2011 (http://www.guardian.co.uk/books/2003/
jan/04/artsfeatures.fiction?INTCMP=SRCH).

Chapel, Jessica. "Sherman Alexie Interview." Atlantic.
com, June 1, 2000. Retrieved August 10, 2011
(http://www.theatlantic.com/past/docs/unbound/
interviews/ba2000-06-01.htm).

Cline, Lynn. "About Sherman Alexie." *Ploughshares*,
Vol. 26, No. 4, Winter 2000/2001, pp. 197-203.

Daley, Lauren. "Novelist Draws on Wellspring of
Experience." SouthCoastToday.com, August 29,
2009. Retrieved August 10, 2011 (http://www
.southcoasttoday.com/apps/pbcs.dll/article?AID=/
20090829/NEWS/908290310&cid=sitesearch).

De Ramirez, Susan Berry Brill. "Fancydancer: A Profile
of Sherman Alexie." *Poets & Writers*, January/
February 1999, pp. 54-59.

Egan, Timothy. "An Indian Without Reservations." *New
York Times*, January 18, 1998.

Grassian, Daniel, ed. *Understanding Sherman Alexie*.
Columbia, SC: University of South Carolina Press,
2005.

Gwinn, Ann. "Identity, Love, and Longing, the Sherman
Alexie Way." *Seattle Times*, October 7, 2009.

"Heroes Now Tend to Be More Hard Edged." *New York
Times*, April 21, 1997.

Jaggi, Maya. "All Rage and Heart." Guardian.co.uk,
May 3, 2008. Retrieved August 6, 2011 (http://
www.guardian.co.uk/books/2008/may/03/
featuresreviews.guardianreview13).

Margolis, Rick. "Song of Myself: Interview with
    Sherman Alexie." SchoolLibraryJournal.com,
    August 1, 2007. Retrieved August 2, 2011
    (http://www.schoollibraryjournal.com/article/
    CA6463515.html).

Maslin, Janet. "Where the Men Are Manly and the Indians
    Bemused." *New York Times*, May 26, 2003.

McNally, Joel. "Sherman Alexie." *Writer*, June 2001, Vol.
    114, No. 6, pp. 26–29.

Mitchell, Elvis. "A Poet Finds His Past Is Just Where He
    Left It." *New York Times*, October 18, 2002.

Nicholls, Richard E. "Skin Games." *New York Times*,
    November 24, 1996.

Nygren, Ase. "A World of Story-Smoke: A Conversation
    with Sherman Alexie." *MELUS*, Vol. 30, No. 4,
    Winter 2005, pp. 149–169.

"Questions for: Sherman Alexie." *New York Times*,
    January 5, 1997.

Ressner, Jeffrey. "Cinema: They've Gotta Have It."
    Time.com, June 29, 1998. Retrieved August 19,
    2011 (http://www.time.com/time/magazine/
    article/0,9171,988633-1,00.html).

Sherman Alexie, interview by Renee Montagne,
    Morning Edition, NPR, September 21, 2007.

"Sherman Alexie: Up All Night." PBS.com, October 4,
    2002. Retrieved August 15, 2011 (http://www
    .pbs.org/now/transcript/transcript_alexie.html).

"Sherman Alexie's Acceptance Speech." NationalBook.
    org, November 14, 2007. Retrieved August 23,
    2011 (http://www.nationalbook.org/audio_video
    .html#sherman).

Skow, John. "Lost Heritage." *Time*, Vol. 148, No. 19, October 21, 1996, p. 88.

Sterngold, James. "Able to Laugh at Their People, Not Just Cry for Them." *New York Times*, June 21, 1998.

Weber, Bruce. "Rhythm and Rhyme of Victory." *New York Times*, June 16, 1998.

West, Dennis. "Sending Cinematic Smoke Signals: An Interview with Sherman Alexie." *Cineaste*, Vol. 23, No. 4, 1998, pp. 28–33.

A

Abenaki Indians, 29
The Absolutely True Diary of a Part-Time Indian, 6–8, 55–62, 64, 65, 73, 78
Adams, Evan, 44
Aerosmith, 77
alcoholism, 14–15, 20, 21, 26–27, 31, 33, 58, 72
Alexie, David, 35
Alexie, Joseph, 35
Alexie, Lillian, 12, 14, 72
Alexie, Sherman (Sr.), 12, 14–15, 18–20, 31, 54
American Indian Film Festival, 45
"American Indians and Alcohol," 15
American Library Association, 58
Animal Farm, 20
Arapaho Indians, 42
Arleo, Adrian, 51
awards, 6, 8, 37, 38, 44, 59, 64, 78

B

basketball, 24, 25, 62, 75–77
Beach, Adam, 44
Before Columbus Foundation American Book Award, 38

binges, drinking, 20
Bird, Gloria, 16
book banning, 58
Boston Globe–Horn Book Award, 59
Boyd, Jim, 36
The Brady Bunch, 75
brain surgery, 9
Bruchac, Joseph, 29
The Business of Fancydancing (book), 31
The Business of Fancydancing (film), 36, 47

C

cartoons, 15, 56
Cheyenne Indians, 42
cirrhosis, 15
Coast Salish Indians, 44
Coeur D'Alene Indians, 12
college, 25, 26–27, 30, 31
Columbia River, 16
Colville Indians, 12, 36
Coyote Springs, 36, 38, 77
creative writing class, 27
critical reception, 31–33, 38, 39–40, 59, 64, 78

D

Dangerous Astronomy, 52

INDEX

Dealey Plaza, 19
Duncan, David James, 51

E

Edge of America, 42
Elliot Bay Book Company, 34
Erdrich, Louise, 72
"Every Teen's Struggle," 23
Eyre, Chris, 42

F

Face, 52, 62
Federal Bureau of
    Investigation (FBI), 53
films, 40–49, 62
First Indian on the Moon, 35
Flathead Indians, 12
Flight, 52–53
Forney, Ellen, 56

G

glasses, 21, 56
Gonzaga University, 25,
    26–27
Granta Top 20 Authors
    Under 40, 70
The Grapes of Wrath, 20, 75
Great Depression, 20

H

Hamlet, 69
Hanging Loose, 30

Harjo, Joh, 29
*Harold and the Purple
    Crayon*, 20
Heavyweight Poetry
    Champion, 75
Hemingway, Ernest, 20
Hershon, Bob, 30
Hidatsa Indians, 35
high school, 21–25, 47, 56
Ho-Chunk Indians, 35
homicide, alcohol-related, 15
Horn Book Magazine, 56,
    64, 65
hydrocephalus, 9, 21, 56

I

Indian Health Service, 21
Indian Killer, 39–40, 45
"An Indian Without
    Reservations," 42–44
insomnia, 15, 20, 66
Institute of American Indian
    Arts, 16
I Would Steal Horses, 31

J

Johnson, Robert, 38
Joseph, Victor, 36, 38, 44

K

Kennedy, John F., 19
kidney failure, 14
King, Stephen, 75

King Lear, 69
Kuo, Alex, 27, 30

L

lisp, 56
Little Bighorn, 52–53
liver disease, 15
The Lone Ranger and Tonto Fistfight in Heaven, 36–38, 40–41
Louis, Adrian C., 8, 29

M

MacLean, Norman, 45
The Magic and Tragic Year of My Broken Thumb, 62
marriage, 35, 73
mascots, sports teams' use of Indians as, 16, 24
Momaday, N. Scott, 72
monoculture, 21

N

National Book Award, 6–8, 59
National Book Foundation, 8
National Institute on Alcohol Abuse and Alcoholism, 15
New York Times Book Review, 33

nonfiction books, 54, 55
Northwest Native American Association, 16
novels, 6–8, 38, 39–40, 52–53, 54–62, 64, 65, 73, 77, 78

O

Ojibwa Indians, 44
Old Shirts and New Skins, 35
One Stick Song, 52
Orwell, George, 20

P

Partridge, Elizabeth, 8
PEN/Faulkner Foundation Award, 64
PEN/Hemingway Award, 38
Ploughshares, 34, 42, 45, 47, 66, 67
poetry, 8, 27–35, 49, 51, 52, 62, 64, 67, 69, 75
Polatkin, Seymour, 47
Potawatomi Indians, 35
public readings, 34
Pullman, 27

R

racism, 58
Radioactive Love Song, 62
Reardan, 54

Reardan High School, 23–25

Reinventing the Enemy's Language: Contemporary Native Women's Writing of North America, 16

Reservation Blues, 36, 38, 45, 77

Reservation Blues: The Soundtrack, 36

reservations, 6, 8, 12–14, 15, 16, 20–21, 23, 24, 25, 29, 38, 44, 52, 53, 56, 47, 61, 65, 69, 70, 72–73, 74

S

screenplays, 40–42, 45

Seattle, 27, 34, 39, 52, 56

seizures, 11–12

serial killer, 39

Seven Mourning Songs for the Cedar Flute I Have Yet to Learn to Play, 35

the "Sherminator," Alexie as, 75

short story collections, 36–38, 40–41, 52, 64, 67

Silko, Leslie, 29, 72

sister, of Sherman Alexie, 14, 34, 57

Skins, 42

smallpox, 16

Smoke Signals, 42–45

Songs from This Earth on Turtle's Back, 27–29

sonnet, 62

Spirit, Arnold, 6–8, 55–57, 59, 62, 65

Spokane Indian Reservation, 6, 8, 12–14, 16, 20–21, 23, 24, 38, 56, 72–73

Spokane Indians, 12, 16, 23, 52, 78–80

Spokane River, 16

Steinbeck, John, 20, 75

stereotypes, 74

suicide, alcohol-related, 15

The Summer of Black Widows, 35

Sundance Film Festival, 44

T

Ten Little Indians, 52

Teters, Charlene, 16

"This Is What It Means to Say Phoenix, Arizona," 41

Thomas Builds-the-Fire, 36, 38, 44

TIME magazine, 40

Tomhave, Diane, 35

Toughest Indian in the World, 52

V

villanelle, 62

violence, 39–40, 53

W

War Dances, 62–64
Washington State
    University, 27, 31
Water Flowing Home, 35
Welch, James, 29
World Poetry Bout, 75
writer's block, 49–51, 66

Y

young adult (YA) literature,
    8, 54–62, 65
Young Men and Fire, 45

Z

Zits, 52–53

ABOUT THE AUTHOR

Liz Sonneborn is a writer living in Brooklyn, New York. A graduate of Swarthmore College, she has written more than eighty books for children, young adults, and adults. Biography and American Indian history and culture are among her specialties. Sonneborn's works include *A to Z of American Indian Women*, *Chronology of American Indian History*, *The American West: An Illustrated History*, *The American Indian Experience*, *Wilma Mankiller*, and *Mark Twain*.

PHOTO CREDITS